*Advice for lovers
first collected in 1850.
This book reveals
the power of love and passion
— for romantics of all ages.*

The
ETIQUETTE
of
LOVE
and
COURTSHIP

Copper Beech Publishing

This edition first published in Great Britain by
Copper Beech Publishing Ltd
© Copyright Copper Beech Publishing Ltd 1995

ISBN 1 898617 05 8

A CIP catalogue record for this book is available from
The British Library.

Editor: Julie Lessels
Cover design: Geoff Gillard

Copper Beech Publishing Ltd
P O Box 159 East Grinstead
Sussex England RH19 4FS

Love

**Be cautious in yielding up the heart to
a worthless object.
Do not choose a partner of a weak capacity.
Look not at a handsome exterior, and
an assumed splendour, but regard
the general deportment of the person on
whom you fix your choice.
If you discover the inward weakness and
incapacity of the individual,
sever the connection, ere it be too late!**

FIRST AFFECTIONS

First affections are the purest and strongest, and if such feelings are met with corresponding feelings and impressions, they are not easily effaced from the mind.

How necessary it is that the utmost caution should be exercised in forming our attachments!

Domestic happiness can be secured by endeavouring to meet with a companion whose disposition, temper and whole deportment will bear the *strictest* scrutiny.

Married life, which ought to be a scene of uninterrupted peace and harmony, can frequently be one of strife and misery.

FALLING IN LOVE

"Falling in love" is an expression which is commonly made use of, but it is an expression which is not altogether admirable.

Love steals upon the feminine heart ...

Numerous and various causes may be mentioned as tending to a person's "falling in love". The female heart is generally soft and tender and is easily susceptible of emotions, which are soon awakened, and wrought upon by flattery and praise.

Impressions are very quickly formed on the mind of a young female, which are not easily effaced; - and at once she gives up her heart to him who has been the cause of awakening those feelings in her mind.

Love steals upon the feminine heart giving a glow and brightness to what was before obscure and dim.

Man ... calculates more carefully

Man, generally, is more upon his guard, and calculates more carefully.

At times, he is so smitten and caught with the beauty and external attractions of a lady at first sight, that in despite of all reason and consideration he is apt to plunge into the abyss of matrimony. But this feeling is *only prevalent* in the heigh-day of youthful love!

Correct knowledge of the *real character* of the lady or gentleman should be possessed by you, before you fix your affections.

Some men ... disguise their real character

Some men are ever ready to disguise their real character and it is no easy matter for a lady to scan it.

He may have all the *traits of a gentleman -*
a handsome exterior, and well skilled in points of etiquette - but these are not sufficient to constitute an agreeable home companion.

It is highly necessary to know something of his disposition, habits and tastes.

If he is disrespectful and disobedient to his parents, or ungentle and unkind to his sisters - this is undeniable evidence, that if he were married, he would manifest a similar disposition!

But should he be kind to his parents, his sisters, and other relatives, he will be so to his wife. The same observations will likewise apply to the females.

Passion ... blind to faults

In bestowing his affections, it is of great importance that suitability of character be taken into consideration, as the happiness of the married state materially depends upon this.

Passion is almost invariably blind to the faults of a lover.

The person on whom you fix your choice, should be *as much as possible* in your own sphere of life.

A man
**of refined taste and of good education,
would not find that degree of happiness,
were he united to a
coarse, vulgar and uncultivated female.**

A lady
**of polished education, and
of fine accomplishments
would feel miserable and uncomfortable,
in having to pass her days in the company
of a boorish, rude
and ignorant husband!**

DISAPPOINTMENT FEEDS THE FIRE OF LOVE

There is nothing that tends so much to fan the flame of love, as the many little trials and disappointments which it has so frequently to contend with.

"The course of true love never did run smooth"

The more love is thwarted and opposed, the more it is strengthened and increased in devotion.

Genuine and unselfish love is never fully established and confirmed, till it has undergone the fiery ordeal of trial and disappointment. When it has been in the furnace, it then attains its highest attribute.

Love laughs at every impediment and overcomes obstacles which seemed almost insurmountable.

"Many waters cannot quench it, neither can the floods drown it."

WOMAN'S LOVE UNSELFISH

Woman must have some object on which to fix her affections - man - and there is but one sort of love, although there are a great number of different copies of it.

She will brave every danger for his sake ...

How frequently is the strength of woman's affection tested, and how seldom has it been found wanting.

She will watch by the couch of him in whom her heart is centred, when sickness and disease have laid him thereon. And when tired nature has worn out every other attendant, she will struggle on, and refuse to leave the side of him whom she loves.

Such is the nature of woman's love - it is pure, it is unselfish.

That man is truly blessed who lives in the embraces of such faithful and unselfish love.

MAN'S LOVE OFTEN SELFISH

Men's motives are frequently very different from those of the softer sex. *Men are too often intent upon gratifying their selfish inclinations* in fixing their choice of companion for life, being influenced by rank, title and dignity.

If they are placed in the middle classes of life, mercenary considerations take a deep hold of their affections!

The dark and crooked paths of cunning ...

The effects of love among men are diversified by their different tempers.

The dark and crooked paths of cunning are unsearchable and inconceivable to an honourable and elevated mind.

When a man blessed with a pure and virtuous disposition is united to a woman of unselfish love, they may truly be said to be happy.

Beneath the dross of outward appearance,
there may often be extracted
metals of the most valuable nature.

QUALITIES REQUISITE IN A LOVER

One individual can discover beauties in an object, at whom another would feel a distaste.

As custom has forbid females that unlimited range in their choice which the men enjoy, so nature has assigned to them a greater flexibility of taste.

Personal beauty is transient and fleeting ...

Indulging in fine words and unmeaning compliments too frequently allures and deceives the fair, but a sincere lover will not hesitate to tell a woman of her failings, rather than flatter her vanity by endeavouring to excuse them.

Personal beauty is transient and fleeting; it endureth but for a short time, and like a flower, its blooms wither after a brief season, and die away.

The inward adorning of the mind is more lasting and endurable.

Disparity in the ages ...

There ought not to be a great disparity in the ages of lovers; if a man has nearly doubled the years of the woman, he will very soon become an old man; ten or a dozen years are commonly considered no very great difference on the man's side.

Marrying for money ...

Much of that unhappiness which is too frequently experienced in a state of wedlock, results from a sordid and selfish desire for riches.

Many parents often render their own and their children's lives miserable by persuading and even compelling them to *marry for money*.

The requisites most essential in a lover are:-

An agreeable person.

Accomplished manners.

Sweetness of temper and disposition.

Free from levity and anything

bordering on the ridiculous.

An unblemished reputation.

A mind stored with virtuous principles.

With a partner of this kind, none need fear to venture upon the stream of matrimony.

PHILANDERING - GENERAL LOVERS

There is a wide distinction between Love and Philandering.

Love exalts and purifies our nature; philandering clouds and debases it.

Love is that prepossession which we feel for a particular person for whose sake we could contentedly give up every other pursuit.

Neither a true friend nor a sincere lover ...

A philandering man can neither be a true friend nor a sincere lover; he can neither give nor receive any lasting satisfaction.

His pleasures are *flat* and *insipid*, because he regards no one woman but as a step to another, and if it were possible for him to subdue them all, he would regret that there were no more to conquer.

Triflers in love ...

The man who obtains the good graces of the woman in general, is seldom worth the regard of any one in particular. These triflers in love, in both sexes, may be justly compared to flies that play about in scalding liquor, till they fall in and lose their life!

It is a great pity, that there are individuals so lost to every sense of shame, as to wish to triumph over the confidence and tenderness of woman - but he frequently meets with his reward.

He often becomes the laughing-stock of every one!

COQUETRY

Of all the people before our observation, the most loathsome is that of the female coquette.

She may not probably have conversation of a respectable order, and may not have read or reflected a deal.

A flirting expedition ...

Pursuits of a literary character are not the relish of a coquette: she will read, if the book be a treatise on washes or cosmetics and if she hopes to find in its pages some advice that will lend aid to her next flirting expedition.

She will peruse an extravagant novel, or romance, because, in so doing, she may imbibe the spirit of chivalry, and reap a lesson from the conduct of the characters in the plot.

Her admirer then lays open his heart and becomes a disgusting fawning idiot!

Those rare qualities of being a good housewife ...

The life of the flaunting coquette, is one continued scene of stratagem and deceit.

Those rare qualities of being a good housewife and economical mistress, are not the butt at which she aims.

A domestic life, in her estimation, is odious; and she quits the sober and diligent services of home, for the flirtings of gaiety, the opera, balls, masquerades, and assemblies, with a thousand other species of amusement, in which she can display her foibles, and be the gazing-stock of the surrounding multitude.

Her dalliance with one excites the other ...

Full of intrigues, deceit, and hypocrisy, she pretends to one what she dissolves next moment in her protestations to another; and thus all are deceived, and yet none desert her standard.

Her dalliance with one, excites the other to strong emotion; and thus she holds in power, at her pleasure, a whole string of the flippant-minded gentlemen.

Home is neglected, and dress and show are courted

A loose, and over-gay conduct in any woman, displays little respect to all those characteristics which make her sex so amiable in the world - whether in the duties of a wife, a parent, a child, a sister, or a friend.

Men are flirted with; true affection becomes a sport; romantic and wild thoughts are cherished.

The principles of good knowledge are despised, for the empty pageantry of a ball-room, or the conversation of a fop; social and domestic acquirements are disregarded as being worthless. Home is neglected, and dress and show are courted.

A wife
**frequently has cause to lament her condition;
but never to utter bitter complaints.**

A husband
**too indulging, is apt to make an impertinent
wife; but unless he be a monster, sweetness of
temper in his wife will restore him to good
humour and soon or late triumph over him.**

CONCLUDING OBSERVATIONS

Love seizes on us suddenly, without giving warning - one look, one glance, fixes and determines us.

Friendship, on the contrary, is a long time in forming, it is of slow growth, through many trials and months of familiarity.

Sweetness of temper ...

Nothing makes a woman more esteemed by the opposite sex, than chastity. The other most important female quality, is sweetness of temper.

Heaven did not give to the female sex insinuation and persuasion, in order to be surly: it did not make them weak, in order to be imperious: it did not give them a sweet voice, in order to be employed in scolding: and it did not provide them with delicate features, in order to be disfigured by anger!

Courtship

**Courtship is a fine bowling-green turf,
all galloping round, and sweet-hearting,
a sunshine holiday in summer time.
But when once through matrimony's turnpike,
the weather becomes wintry!**

PRELIMINARY REMARKS - GENTLEMEN

There is something in the very nature of woman which ignites in man *flames of passion.*

She has been formed with a gentler and less uncouth mien. She possesses all the qualities of virtue, beauty is in her form, and tenderness in her look; delicacy sits upon her cheek; love heaves beneath her breast; and there is a helplessness - a softness - which calls forth the esteem of man.

A little experience will cure ... imperfections

It requires great care to carry out an attachment through the medium of courtship.

Love causes a young man to *speak and act in a ridiculous manne*r even in the presence of her whom he loves.

A little experience will cure him of many imperfections and enable him to act in a more rational and becoming manner.

*Courtship is matrimony's running footman,
but seldom stays to see the stocking thrown;
it is often carried away by
the two grand preservatives of matrimonial
friendship, delicacy and gratitude.*

Females ... quick in discerning weak points

Young men should be very careful how they conduct themselves in the presence of the ladies. To brag and bluster before them is one of the greatest acts of folly and imprudence of which you can be guilty.

Females in general, are very quick in discerning the weak points in character.

They form their opinions and judgements according to the conduct which you practise in their presence.

Unworthy of her acquaintance ...

Some men are very much addicted to the folly of speaking of their connections; this shows a weak and puerile mind and every sensible lady will consider the person unworthy of her acquaintance.

There are those young men who imagine that because they receive from a lady that courtesy and kindness which *good breeding* prompts, that the lady is in love with them. This is a great and serious mistake; and is dishonourable to the man.

*To waste our precious moments
in the embroidery of the person
and to neglect the cultivation of the mind,
is to foster pride, selfishness and conceit.*

ON DRESS

Good sense and refined taste ...

It will be very difficult to lay down any fixed rules with regard to your dress.

Fashion is ever-changing, and in this matter you should be guided by good sense and refined taste. It is necessary that you should dress neat according to your station; but not endeavour to imitate those who are in a higher sphere of life.

The love of dress leads on to extravagance ...

High life is full of changes. We know very well that men do not always act with prudence, and consider before they engage themselves in debt, whether or not they have a sufficiency to extricate themselves when called upon for their just owings. It consequently adds to the necessity of guarding against the indulgence of young and inexperienced inclinations.

Satisfy the passion for show and gaiety ...

Dress has bearings upon the mind; to satisfy the passion for show and gaiety, is to warp every virtuous principle, and will eventually lead on to ruin and poverty.

Taste and discernment ...

If the lady to whom you are paying your addresses is possessed of *taste* and *discernment,* you will act properly in submitting to her judgement with regard to your dress.

THE GENTLEMAN'S PROPOSAL TO THE LADY

Whenever a gentleman is so influenced with love, it is certainly time for him to decide how he is to make known to her his sentiments in such a manner as shall be in accordance with *strict* propriety and decorum.

Apply to the lady's parents ...

If he has any just reason to think that the lady will not object to his suit, then the most proper course to pursue in the commencement is for him to apply to the lady's parents or guardians for their consent to his paying his addresses to her.

Should there by any objection on the part of the parents or guardians of the lady, you can solace your mind by reflecting that you have in no way wilfully neglected those observances which etiquette deems honourable and respectful on such occasions.

Imprudent conduct ...

It is sometimes however, the case in matters of love, that an attachment is formed almost unconsciously and imperceptibly - that the heart is taken captive and an exchange of mutual regard and affection is commenced before the parties ever dreamt of any other preliminaries, which should have preceded such an engagement. *Every one ought carefully to guard against such imprudent conduct!*

Path of courtship ... smooth and tranquil

Should a gentleman sustain a much higher station in life than the lady whom he is about to espouse, it is his duty to communicate to his own parents or guardians how he stands affected to the object of his choice.

If they approve of that choice, they will acquaint the parents or guardians of the lady with their approval, and thus the path of courtship will be smooth and tranquil.

THE GENTLEMAN'S OFFER NOT ACCEPTED

Although a lady has not the advantage of proposing love to any gentleman, she has the authority of accepting or refusing any proposition of love.

Sneers and ridicule ...

There are ladies who are disposed to trifle and sport with the feelings of a desponding swain, after he has had a firm denial.

A man of taciturn habits, fell in love with a girl, who was addicted to gaiety in dress and disposition!

She strongly objected to his offers, yet he still persisted to tease her. She did not altogether abandon him, but appeared at times to treat him with favour and encouragement - occasionally smiling upon him in a gracious manner.

He could not see through her artifice, *but continued to dangle after her;* and exposed himself to the sneers and ridicule of the town!

Monarchs
are certainly not permitted
to choose for themselves,
in matrimonial alliances.

Their subjects have a right to this privilege.
It is their bounden duty to exercise it,
as much of their future happiness depends
upon the choice of a partner.

REFUSAL OF THE LADY'S PARENTS

Unhappy marriages may be occasioned by the determined opposition manifested by parents.

Unhappiness caused by haste and rashness ...

Much unhappiness in the married state may have been caused by the haste and rashness of young people in entering into engagements without due consideration and prudence.

A Gretna Green marriage ...

We are averse to clandestine courtships or marriages under any circumstances whatever. A Gretna Green marriage will soon subside into a persuasion that will in no way elevate the reputations of the pair. Yet at times the opposition is so cruel and unprincipled, that young persons may be justified in uniting themselves together in matrimony without the consent of parents or guardians.

THE GENTLEMAN'S OFFER ACCEPTED

The young lover, when he has got the consent of the lady must be very careful, and exercise prudence and caution in discharging those little duties and requirements so necessary in a successful courtship.

Do not be always dangling at the skirt of your fair mistress ...

You must be very nice and exact in your behaviour before the object of your choice.

Your attentions should only go so far as prudence requires - *excess often disgusts.* Do not be always dangling at the skirt of your fair mistress. Be moderate in your attendance upon her; - and when in her company, *let your conversation be dictated by wisdom and sound judgement.*

Because you are introduced into the family as a suitor, it does not follow that you are entitled to any other freedom or liberty not formerly possessed.

Your engagement may be terminated; and it is still uncertain whether you will become one of the family or not.

Beware of unmeaning flirting ...

If your attachment is based on sound and virtuous principles, and the lady is in possession of similar feelings, be careful to value such an object.

We urgently advise you to beware of unmeaning flirting. That unnatural system of flirtation with other ladies, is surely the greatest folly and calculated to create distrust and suspicion in the mind of your lover.

You may indulge in this reprehensible conduct under the idea that it is merely an *innocent* pastime, but be assured, that it often leads to *serious* consequences. A young lady who may be thus treated by him in whom she has confided, should discard her flirting swain, and never speak to him more!

THE GENTLEMAN'S CONDUCT TO THE LADY IN PUBLIC

Acting imprudently ... stains your character

A great amount of care and circumspection is required in a lover with regard to his conduct to his "lady love" in public.

Acting imprudently on these occasions, not only stains your character with degradation, but that of your betrothed also; and it is very easy for you both to be exposed to the sarcasm and criticism of the world.

We would not deter any young man from paying to the fair sex that attention which etiquette demands, *but never overstep the bounds of reason and moderation.* Ever aim to give your chief attention to her who has the greatest right to it.

An indifferent behaviour and inattention to the wishes of your partner will necessarily lead her to suspect the sincerity of your love!

Differences may take place between lovers;
but refrain from speaking in public ...

Let not anger or resentment
have a place in your bosom.

Divulge not to a third person
the unhappy state of affairs
betwixt you and your mistress.

Endeavour by all justifiable and
honourable means to heal the breach,
and to become reconciled to your lover.

Never indulge too freely in proclaiming
the charms of your partner.

Weakness and folly ...

We would caution you against showing your weakness and folly in appearing to be jealous when your lover receives the common civilities and courtesies from another young man, which *good-breeding* warrants.

Bear in mind that her being engaged to you, does not deprive her of receiving that respectful attention from other gentlemen which the rules of etiquette sanction.

Numerous engagements have been broken, by harbouring a feeling of petty jealousy, without any just occasion.

A young lady who was thus treated by her lover, dismissed him; and thanked him that he had shown her his true character before marriage!

CONDUCT OF THE GENTLEMAN ON
BEING DISMISSED FROM HIS ENGAGEMENT

It may occur in courtship that the lady sees reason for declining to continue her engagement with you. When this is the case, we would advise you to act in a becoming manner.

Etiquette forbids any vindictive or dishonourable behaviour ...

If her objections are based on reason and justice and not on caprice, accede at once, however painful the stroke may be, to her request.

Conduct yourself towards her as a gentleman; and submit with fortitude and resignation to the separation. Censure her not in public: *betray no secrets* which she may have confided to you: reveal nothing which may have occurred in the course of your courtship, even to your most intimate friends.

Should the lady break off her engagement without giving a just and sufficient reason for her conduct, still we would advise you to refrain from manifesting any kind of harshness; - you may pity her, but etiquette forbids you showing any vindictive or dishonourable behaviour; - or retaliating in any unbecoming manner.

Return letters and presents ...

It is usual to return each other's letters, presents, and other mementoes of affection, which may have been bestowed or received.

CONDUCT OF THE GENTLEMAN ON BREAKING OFF HIS ENGAGEMENT

When a gentleman feels desirous to discontinue his attentions, he will be placed in a far more difficult position than a lady who is anxious to retreat from her engagement.

The gentlest language you can adopt ...

He may have so far secured her affections, that to disappoint her, may be fatal to her happiness and her life.

If you should ever be placed in such a situation, exercise the utmost delicacy and tenderness. Should your reasons for severing the connection arise from any seeming improprieties in her conduct, you should endeavour to convey to her the state of your mind in the gentlest language that you can adopt.

Do not wish to irritate her, but use soothing accents, in giving her a knowledge of your determination.

PROPOSAL OF MARRIAGE

After a proper time for courtship, and all parties being amicably disposed to one another, marriage is the important step which you wish to take.

Etiquette requires that you make known your wishes to the lady's parents or guardians; your own also being fully acquainted with your intentions.

The preliminary arrangements with regard to fortune is a delicate subject, but circumstances must guide you on the occasion.

Let candour and generosity actuate you in this difficult transaction.

GENERAL REMARKS TO LADIES

Our remarks have been hitherto confined to gentlemen; we shall now address the other sex; and our observations will be brief. For we must acknowledge, that the science or etiquette of courtship is *even more difficult and delicate* with ladies than with gentlemen.

The rude attacks of designing men ...

Modesty in the female sex is ever the attendant of innocence, and is a bright ornament wherever it is cherished and practised to its fullest extent.

Whilst you are exposed to the rude attacks of designing men, be careful and circumspect in your deportment.

Pride is essential to dignity of character, but haughty and arrogant pride is a vice which is detestable.

Some females are much addicted to flirtation; but such conduct often terminates in disappointment and remorse.

CONDUCT OF THE LADY ON A PROPOSAL OF LOVE

Great caution and circumspection are necessary when a gentleman first discloses his sentiments to you.

Prudence and discretion are absolutely necessary ...

Should his person be agreeable to you, and there are no objections with regard to his character and worldly prospects, there will not be much difficulty in your coming to a decision.

Your wisest plan ...

Should the proposition *not* be in accordance with your feelings, your wisest plan will be to refer the gentleman to your parents or guardians, acquainting them with your objections, who will inform the gentleman of the decision you have come to.

Rank and station ...

Much importance is attached to rank and station in life. This ought to have some influence on your mind in the choice of a partner.

Were you to marry a man much beneath you in point of rank, you would *at once* sink yourself to the position he occupies, whereas should you marry a man in a higher sphere than you sustain in society, you are thus elevated to his position.

> *It is not the rank of the lady*
> *that raises the husband,*
> *but that of the gentleman that elevates*
> *the lady to his standard!*

CONDUCT OF THE LADY TOWARDS HER LOVER

Avoid too much familiarity ...

At the commencement of youthful love, there is a propensity to overstep the limits of prudence and to rush into excess. Such conduct must be carefully refrained from on the lady's part. She must ever avoid too much familiarity.

If you are anxious for him to have a high regard of your love, lavish it not too freely and foolishly on him!

Show not the extent of your love ...

You have already given proof of a special regard for your lover; he ought not to expect more. Show not the extent of your love; but maintain your character for independence.

Etiquette forbids you from showing too much concern for him to whom you are betrothed.

There are ladies who, when in company, (and expecting their lovers), have manifested restless dispositions until they have arrived: *this conduct is very unbecoming.*

Show not by any outward sign your anxiety, but be calm and tranquil; and when your lover arrives receive him with politeness and respect.

Let your conversation with him be dictated by sound sense, and on the common topics of every day occurrence.

It ought ever to be borne in mind by a lady, that a gentleman seldom attaches much value on that it has cost him nothing to gain as his possession!

When in public ...

There are young ladies who take pleasure in prom-
enading with their lovers on every available occasion.
This is not in strict accordance with the etiquette of
good breeding.

Some young ladies have lost their lovers by too
freely exhibiting them!

Calm and persuasive language ...

The attentions of a lady should be equally dispensed
when in the company of gentlemen.

Should the folly and weakness of your lover betray
him into such indiscretion as to make both you and
himself ridiculous in company, strongly remonstrate
with him on the impropriety of his conduct in calm and
persuasive language.

Your lover expects ... preference in your attentions

You should by no means neglect all the little courtesies and polite attentions of gentlemen on account of

your being engaged to another. This would be a breach of true politeness.

Never be betrayed into too great a freedom. Your lover expects, and certainly has a right to a preference in your attentions; and if you be too lavish of them, you expose yourself to the imputation of being a flirt!

Jokes ...

Be careful how far you exercise your humour in passing jokes upon your lover. This conduct discovers a levity of character which does not altogether consist with pure and devoted attachment!

If your lover be of a weak and irritable disposition, you are certainly not required to indulge such a temperament; but you should endeavour in a mild, calm and dignified manner, to reprove him for giving way to such weakness.

CONDUCT OF THE LADY ON DECLINING HER ENGAGEMENT WITH THE GENTLEMAN

If you discover traits in a gentleman's character and disposition which lead you to believe that you could not enjoy happiness with him, then you will be justified in breaking off your engagement.
Etiquette indeed forbids you to continue it any longer.

Men who are the most abject flatterers ...

Many men accustom themselves in courtship to a behaviour suitable for the occasion, which continues during the honeymoon, and then disappears!

They will be everything which pleases the ladies, who are thus deceived and expect the same behaviour through life. By and by they discover their mistake, and instead of being treated like goddesses, they are merely used as women!

Men who are the most abject flatterers generally degenerate into the most cruel tyrants.

CONDUCT OF THE LADY
ON THE GENTLEMAN BREAKING OFF HIS
ENGAGEMENT

It is an unpleasant situation for a gentleman when he is discarded, yet it is still more so for a lady to be severed from an engagement in which she had cherished the hope of enjoying years of happiness.

If the gentleman, in breaking off his engagement, behave himself in an unbecoming manner, the lady should so far control her feelings as to treat him with civility; by acting in this manner she will maintain her dignity and self-respect.

It is difficult to devise a plan for individuals in such cases, but the usual course is to refer the case to parents or guardians and leave them to arrange and settle the matter.

CONDUCT OF THE LADY IN THE CHOICE OF HER COMPANIONS

A lady's conduct in courtship very much depends on the person whom she chooses as her *confidante*. A female will not be so silly as to have a number of friends to whom she will open her heart and reveal her sentiments; but it is natural that you should single out some sympathising soul, in whom you can repose your confidence without suspicion.

A friend may be of great service to you ...

Relatives are the persons most proper, as they naturally feel a deeper interest in your welfare than other people. But if you cannot place confidence in any of your relatives, be *very cautious* to whom you intrust a knowledge of your affairs. Your friend may be of great service to you, if she is possessed of honest and upright principles.

CORRESPONDENCE

"Our thoughts, our wishes, and our doubts
We can more freely write,
Than utter with our tongues to those
In whom we take delight."

Letter writing is of far greater importance than most people are aware.

Before you begin a sentence ...

A woman who begins a speech or letter, before she has determined what to say, will undoubtedly find herself bewildered before she gets to the end.

To avoid this, before you begin a sentence have the whole of it in your head. Make use of the first words that offer themselves to express your meaning, they are the most natural, and will, generally speaking, best answer your purpose.

Candour and sincerity ...

Be careful that you make use of no expressions that may be derogatory to your character. Write the sentiments of your mind with candour and sincerity; and though you may be strongly attached to your lover, refrain from expressing the ardency of your love to him.

If he be one devoid of principle ...

You should ever remember that your engagement may be dissolved; and though it is usually expected that all letters are returned; you may be disappointed in that expectation.

The gentleman with whom you have corresponded, may have taken copies of your letters, and if he be one devoid of principle, he will take a pleasure in *showing your letters to other people.*

Therefore make use of no sentiments or expressions in your letters which you will have occasion to be ashamed of.

A plain style ... fixes an impression

Express your meaning as freely as possible. A short plain style strikes the mind and fixes an impression, a tedious one is seldom understood.

But there is still something requisite towards the writing of an agreeable letter and that is *an air of good breeding*.

Other books in this series:

THE ETIQUETTE OF AN ENGLISH TEA
For tea lovers everywhere.
How to serve a perfect English afternoon tea;
tea traditions, superstitions, recipes - including
how to read your fortune in the
tea-leaves afterwards.

THE ETIQUETTE OF POLITENESS
Good sense and good manners.
How to be polite and well-bred at all times.

ETIQUETTE FOR GENTLEMEN
Rules for perfect conduct.
For the gentleman in every woman's life!

For your free catalogue containing these and other
Copper Beech Gift Books, write to:

Copper Beech Publishing Ltd
P O Box 159 East Grinstead Sussex England RH19 4FS

Copper Beech Gift Books
are designed and printed
in Great Britain